Novels for Students, Volume 27

Project Editor: Ira Mark Milne Rights Acquisition and Management: Vernon English, Leitha Etheridge-Sims, Aja Perales, Sue Rudolph Composition: Evi Abou-El-Seoud Manufacturing: Drew Kalasky

Imaging: Lezlie Light

Product Design: Pamela A. E. Galbreath, Jennifer Wahi Content Conversion: Civie Green, Katrina Coach Product Manager: Meggin Condino © 2008 Gale, Cengage Learning

For product information and technology assistance, contact us at **Gale Customer Support, 1-800-877-4253.**

For permission to use material from this text or product, submit all requests online at **www.cengage.com/permissions.**

Further permissions questions can be emailed to **permissionrequest@cengage.com** While every effort has been made to ensure the reliability of the information presented in this publication, Gale, a part of Cengage Learning, does not guarantee the accuracy of the data contained herein. Gale accepts no payment for listing; and inclusion in the publication of any organization, agency, institution, publication, service, or individual does not imply endorsement of the editors or publisher. Errors brought to the attention of the publisher and verified to the satisfaction of the publisher will be corrected in future editions.

Gale
27500 Drake Rd.
Farmington Hills, MI, 48331-3535

ISBN-13: 978-0-7876-8684-0
ISBN-10: 0-7876-8684-0
ISSN 1094-3552

This title is also available as an e-book.

ISBN-13: 978-1-4144-3831-3
ISBN-10: 1-4144-3831-1
Contact your Gale, a part of Cengage Learning sales
representative for ordering information.

Printed in the United States of America
1 2 3 4 5 6 7 12 11 10 09 08

My Name is Red

Orhan Pamuk 2001

Introduction

My Name Is Red is a novel by Turkish writer Orhan Pamuk, who won the Nobel Prize for Literature in 2006. Set in Istanbul, the capital city of the powerful Ottoman Empire, in 1591, the novel functions at many different levels. Covering a period of about a week, it is at once a murder mystery, a love story, and an examination of the cultural tensions between East and West. These tensions center around different theories of art. The Ottoman Sultan has commissioned an illustrated book to celebrate the power of his empire, and he has ordered that the paintings employ the techniques of the Italian Renaissance, in which the use of perspective and shadow create realistic portraits that are quite different from the stylized representations of Islamic tradition. The use of the new style creates fear amongst the artists commissioned to produce the book, and two murders are the result. Black, an artist who has just returned to Istanbul and is courting the beautiful Shekure, is told by the Sultan that he must solve the case within three days or he and the other master artists will be tortured. With its theme of East-West conflict, and its examination of what happens when Western ideas creep into a restrictive Islamic society, *My Name Is Red*, although set four hundred years ago, has much relevance for the cultural conflicts of today.

A recent edition of the story, translated from the Turkish by Erdağ M. Göknar, was released by Vintage International in 2002.

Author Biography

Orhan Pamuk was born in Istanbul, Turkey, on June 7, 1952, and grew up in a large family in a wealthy area of the city. When he was a child he acquired an interest in painting and wanted to become an artist, a desire he entertained until he was in his early twenties.

Pamuk graduated from the American Robert College in Istanbul and studied architecture for three years at Istanbul Technical University. But he decided not to pursue his earlier goals of becoming an artist or architect and instead turned to journalism. He graduated from the Institute of Journalism at the University of Istanbul in 1976. However, he never pursued a career in journalism. Instead, at the age of twenty-three, he decided to become a novelist. For the next seven years, he lived with his parents, who supported his writing.

Pamuk's first novel, *Cevdet Bey ve ogullari: roman*, was published in 1982. It is the story of three generations of a wealthy family living in Istanbul. Pamuk then wrote *Sessiz ev: roman* (1983). His third novel, *Beyaz kale: roman* (1985), was translated into English and published as *The White Castle: A Novel* (1990 in England, 1991 in the United States). About the interaction between East and West in Istanbul, the novel earned Pamuk an international reputation.

Pamuk was a visiting scholar at Columbia

University, New York, from 1985 to 1988. During this time he wrote most of his next novel, *Kara Kitap*, which was published in Turkey in 1990 and in the United States in 1994 as *The Black Book*. *Yeni hayat* (1994) was translated as *The New Life* (1997).

Benim Adim Kirmizi (2000) was translated from Turkish and first published as *My Name Is Red* in the United States in 2001. The novel won the French Prix Du Meilleur Livre Étranger (2001), the Italian Grinzane Cavour (2002) and the prestigious International IMPAC Dublin literary award (2003).

Kar (2002) published in English as *Snow* (2002), which Pamuk described as the only political novel he has written, is about tensions between political Islamists, secularists, and Kurdish and Turkish nationalists.

Over the years, Pamuk has been critical of the Turkish government over human rights issues, and in 2005, he was subjected to criminal charges over remarks he made in an interview with a Swiss magazine. Pamuk commented that thirty thousand Kurds had been killed in the conflict between Kurdish nationalists and Turkish security forces, and that a million Armenians were killed in Turkey in 1915, but that no one spoke about it.

After an international outcry, the charges against Pamuk were dropped in January 2006. He has subsequently stated that his intent in making the controversial statements was to draw attention to freedom of expression issues in Turkey.

In 2006, Pamuk was awarded the 2006 Nobel Prize in literature. In the same year, he was appointed visiting professor at Columbia University. As of 2007, Pamuk is a Fellow with Columbia University's Committee on Global Thought.

Plot Summary

Chapters 1-10

Set in a winter in Istanbul in 1591, *My Name Is Red* is told in brief chapters by multiple narrators; the narrator is identified in the heading of each chapter. Chapter 1 is told by a murdered man whose as-yet-undiscovered-corpse lies at the bottom of a well. His name was Elegant and he was an artist working on illustrations for a secret book commissioned by the Sultan.

Chapter 2 is narrated by Black, who has just returned to Istanbul after a twelve-year absence. For all that time he has been in love with his cousin, Shekure. He is returning to Istanbul at the invitation of his uncle, Enishte, to whom he was formerly apprenticed. Enishte is also an artist, and it is he who is in charge of preparing the secret book for the Sultan. Enishte has asked Black for assistance, since Black has experience commissioning artists. Black walks the streets of Istanbul and enters a coffeehouse, in which a storyteller has hung a picture of a dog. He is giving voice to the dog and pointing at the drawing. The next chapter is narrated by the dog. He questions why some people dislike dogs.

Chapter 4 is narrated by the man who murdered Elegant, although he does not identify himself. He is also in the coffeehouse, and he reveals that, he, like Elegant, is a miniaturist. He discusses what it feels like to be a murderer and reveals that Elegant had believed the illustrations they were doing were heretical. The murderer feared that they would all be denounced to the fundamentalists.

Chapter 5 is narrated by Enishte, Black's uncle, who recalls the circumstances of Black's departure, twelve years ago. This happened because Black fell in love with Enishte's daughter, Shekure, but was not considered a suitable match, so he was asked to leave the house. Several years later, Shekure married a cavalryman and had two children. But her husband, after going off to war, has now been missing for four years. Enishte tells Black that the portrait of the Sultan that is to be included in the secret book will be painted in the Venetian style, as a genuine portrait of the man. This will be a departure from the impersonal style of the Islamic miniaturists.

Chapter 6 is told by Orhan, Shekure's six-year-old son. Orhan overhears his grandfather telling Black that he thinks Elegant was murdered because of the controversial nature of his work, even though Elegant worked in the old style. Orhan and his brother Shevket misbehave and their mother makes them wait in the kitchen until Black leaves.

Black takes up the story in chapter 7. He relates his feelings on visiting Enishte's house. He desperately wants to see Shekure again. Enishte tells him he must visit all the miniaturists working on the book, as well as Master Osman, the Head

Illuminator. As he rides away, a clothes peddler named Esther hands him a letter from Shekure, and he also catches a glimpse of Shekure's face in the window.

In chapter 8, Esther, who delivers letters as she hawks her wares around the city, relates how she came to deliver the letter to Black. She knows that Shekure has told Black not to return. Esther guesses, however, that Shekure does not mean what she says.

Shekure tells her own story in chapter 9. She confirms Esther's intuition that she does not want to discourage Black, and also tells the story of how she fell in love with her husband. After he went missing, she had to move back in with her father. She knows that Hasan, her brother-in-law, wants to marry her, but she does not want to marry him.

Chapter 10 is told by a tree, which says it does not want to be depicted in the Western, Venetian style, like a real tree. Instead, it wants to reveal what the meaning of a tree is.

Chapters 11-20

Black is the narrator in chapter 11. He reads Shekure's letter and dreams of being married. In the morning he visits the royal artisans' workshop, and senses that Master Osman is suspicious of him. Osman reveals that the miniaturists Olive, Stork, and Butterfly work on the special book—not at the workshop but at home. Black is given a tour of the workshop, and on his way back he gives Esther a letter for Shekure.

The next three chapters are related by, respectively, Butterfly, Stork, and Olive. Each artist receives a visit from Black, who questions them about their philosophical approach to art and looks at some of their paintings. Each artist tells three stories that allude to the matter of artistic style (Butterfly), the nature of painting and time (Stork), and blindness and memory (Olive). Black observes everything in their homes, searching for any clue to Elegant's disappearance. News arrives that Elegant's body has been found.

Chapters 15 and 16, narrated by Esther and Shekure respectively, return to the love story of Black and Shekure. Esther visits Hasan and shows him the letter Black has written to Shekure, in which he says he wants to marry her. Hasan, who also wants Shekure, gives Esther a letter he has written to Shekure. He asks Esther what he can do to convince Shekure and her father that he would make a suitable husband. Shekure is confused by the situation.

In chapter 17, Enishte tells of his attendance at Elegant's funeral. Butterfly tells him that the miniaturists were jealous of one another over who would assume leadership of the workshop after Master Osman died. Butterfly admits that he had a bad relationship with Elegant, but believes Olive and Stork are exploiting this in order to blame him for the murder.

Chapter 18 is narrated by the murderer, who

attended Elegant's funeral and wept more than anyone else at the graveside. Chapter 19 is told by a gold coin, which narrates its travels across Istanbul.

The story returns to Black's viewpoint. He listens to Enishte speak of the portraits he had seen in Venice, where portraiture is popular amongst the affluent. Enishte is both attracted to the portraits and appalled by them.

Chapters 21-30

In chapter 21 (told from Enishte's point of view), Enishte explains to Black how he had persuaded the Sultan to fund the secret book, and that the last picture was nearly finished. He shows Black a picture of Death, painted by Butterfly, and all the other illustrations to the book. Black goes home thinking of Shekure, believing that she was watching him while he visited her father. He contemplates the task Enishte has given him, which is to write a story to accompany each illustration in the book, and he knows he must do this if he is to win Shekure.

In chapter 23, which is narrated by the murderer, the culprit describes how tormented he is following the murder. He reveals that he is also in love with Shekure. In the next chapter, Death reveals that the miniaturist who was persuaded by Enishte to illustrate Death regrets his decision because in painting the picture, he was unwittingly imitating the Frankish (Western) method.

Esther narrates how, in a letter, Shekure tells

Black that he must complete the manuscript if he is to win her love. Black asks her to meet him at an abandoned house.

In chapter 26, Shekure tells of reading Hasan's letter, in which he says that he is going to the judge in order to force her to live with him. Shekure ignores Hasan's letter but agrees to meet Black at the abandoned house. When they meet, they embrace and kiss. In chapter 27, Black agrees to testify that he has seen the corpse of her husband, so that she can be declared a widow and be free to marry him.

Chapter 28 is narrated by the murderer, who visits Enishte and tells him about the rumors that the book they are preparing is blasphemous. He is worried about the final illustration and fears it is painted in the Frankish style. Enishte replies that two styles can be brought together to create something new. But the two men grow suspicious of each other, and then the murderer confesses that he killed Elegant.

The narration is taken up by Enishte in chapter 29, who fears that the murderer will kill him, too. After a lengthy discussion about the nature of painting, the murderer hits him on the head with an ink pot, killing him.

Shekure narrates how, when she comes home, (Chapter 30) she discovers her father's body. She moves it into a back room and tells the children that their grandfather is sleeping. She informs Hayrire of the murder but tells her to behave as if nothing has happened.

Chapters 31-40

After chapter 31 is narrated by the color red, Shekure continues the story. She tells Black she wants to conceal Enishte's death because otherwise Hasan and his father will be appointed her guardians. She says that she will marry Black, but until the murderer is caught and the Sultan's book is finished, she will not share his bed. Chapter 32 is then narrated by Black, who bribes the authorities to grant Shekure a divorce. At the wedding ceremony, the dead Enishte is dressed in nightclothes, as if he were sick, so he can act as Shekure's guardian.

After the wedding, Shekure and Black agree, in chapter 34 (told by Shekure), to announce in the morning that Enishte has died in his sleep. Shekure awakes during the night, goes outside and finds Hasan and Black arguing. Hasan claims the marriage is invalid. He also claims that Shekure, in league with Black, killed her father. He says he will forgive her if she returns to live with him. Black responds by accusing Hasan of killing Enishte.

Chapter 35 is narrated by a horse, who argues in favor of the Frankish style of painting. In the morning, Shekure announces Enishte's death. Black gets an audience with the Head Treasurer and tells him that he suspects the secret book Enishte was working on was the cause of his murder because it fostered jealousy among the artists.

In chapter 37, the dead Enishte tells of his

public funeral, which was attended by many dignitaries. He says his soul is at peace. Chapter 38 is narrated by Master Osman, who is summoned to a meeting with the Head Treasurer and the Commander of the Imperial Guard. The Head Treasurer says the Sultan is furious that Enishte has been murdered. He wants the book finished and the murderer caught. Black, Olive, Stork, and Butterfly are all suspects. The Commander says he is authorized to torture Black and the others if necessary during interrogation.

Chapter 39 is narrated by Esther. Esther visits the widow of Elegant, who informs her of some sketches of horses that were found with the body of her husband. Since Elegant did not draw horses, they might be the work of the murderer. In chapter 40, Black tells readers that he is summoned to the palace, where he is tortured. He denies knowing anything of Elegant's murder, and Master Osman informs him that the torture was only a test. But Osman also informs him that unless he finds the murderer within three days, as well as the missing final illustration, he will be the first to be tortured.

Chapters 41-50

Master Osman tells of how he and Black examine illustrations from the secret book to determine which miniaturist illustrated which one. Osman dislikes the pictures and has no desire to finish the book. With Black, Osman discusses the talents and temperaments of Olive, Butterfly, and

Stork. He reveals that he favors Butterfly to succeed him as leader of the workshop because he is the only one who could resist the lure of Venetian artistry.

In chapter 42, narrated by Black, Shekure's letter enclosing the sketches of the horses is delivered to the palace, where Master Osman and Black receive it. They try to match the sketches to an illustration of a horse in the secret book, concluding that they were drawn by the same hand. They notice that the horse's nostrils are drawn oddly. It is a clue as to which miniaturist might have drawn the picture. They examine hundreds of other horses painted by Butterfly, Stork, and Olive, but none of them bear this peculiarity. Master Osman suggests to the Sultan that they ask each miniaturist to draw a horse quickly and say it is for a contest.

In chapters 43-45, Olive, Butterfly, and Stork respectively narrate how they were asked to draw a horse to see who could draw the best horse in the shortest time. They describe their technique. In chapter 46, the murderer reveals that he knew it was not a competition, and that the authorities wanted to catch him. However, he believes he has no peculiarity of style that will betray him.

Chapter 47 is narrated by Satan, who has just been identified by the murderer as the being who first separated East and West by asserting his own individuality and thus, in artistic terms, adopting a particular style. But Satan refutes this argument, which is also put forward by the fundamentalists.

Chapter 48 returns to Shekure's point of view. She has doubts about her decision to marry Black. Black tries to reassure her by saying how much he loves her. Black (in chapter 49) goes to the palace, where Master Osman tells him that they are unable to determine from the three horse illustrations who drew the horse in the sketches found on Elegant. Osman persuades the Sultan to allow him to examine centuries-old books in the Treasury to find out whether the unusual depiction of the horse's nose is a mistake or whether it reflects other techniques from the past. They examine thousands of pictures.

Chapter 50 is related by two dervishes, characters in a painting over one hundred years old rendered in the Venetian style.

Chapters 51-59

In chapter 51, Master Osman relates how he spends the entire night in the Treasury with Black studying thousands of illustrations. He feels deep affection for all the masters of old, and he relives with delight all the years he has labored as a painter. He knows that the artistic world he knew is coming to an end. After studying the legendary *Book of Kings*, he finds the needle that the great master Bihzad had used to blind himself. Knowing that he cannot prevent the spread of the new method of painting, Osman presses the needle into his eyes, which means he will soon go blind.

Chapter 52 is narrated by Black, who discovers

in an album a picture of a horse with peculiar nostrils and takes it to Osman. Osman identifies the nose as resembling the noses of Mongol horses, who had their nostrils cut open. It is painted in the Chinese style. Osman then says he thinks Olive is the one who drew the horses in Enishte's book, because he is the one who best knows the old styles. But he does not believe Olive is the murderer, because both Olive and Elegant were devoted to the old methods. Osman believes the murderer was Stork. Black is confused, and even suspects that Osman orchestrated the murders. As he leaves the Treasury he takes with him the needle that Bihzad and Osman used to blind themselves.

Chapter 53 is narrated by Esther, who receives a visit from Black. She informs him that Shekure's former husband is on his way back and that Shekure and her sons are now living at Hasan's home. Black and some armed men go to the house. Hasan is not at home so Black sends Shekure a note. Esther notes how confused she is, ready to love either Black or Hasan if either of them prove to be a good father to her boys. She finds out that the former husband is not really returning; that was Hasan's lie. Black and his men attack the house although they do not enter it. Eventually Shekure agrees to return to live with Black.

After a chapter narrated by a man who dresses as a woman, the story returns to Butterfly's point of view in chapter 55. Butterfly reports an attack by the followers of a fundamentalist preacher on a coffeehouse. On his way back, Butterfly is accosted by Black, who presses a dagger to his throat. Black forces Butterfly back to Butterfly's house, telling him he is going to search it. He wants to find the final, missing illustration. At the house, Butterfly turns the tables on Black, pinning him to the ground and threatening to kill him. Butterfly is worried that Stork and Olive are conspiring against him, and he convinces Black to accompany him to Olive's house. Olive is not at home.

In chapter 56, narrated by Stork, they arrive at Stork's house, ransack his possessions and quiz him about which miniaturist drew certain pictures for the storyteller in the coffeehouse. Eventually they all decide to join forces, since they are scared of Master Osman and the tortures they may all face, and they find Olive at a dervish lodge. Chapter 57 is narrated by Olive, who claims he was not the one who drew the horse with the peculiar nostrils, but Black and Stork search his rooms anyway. Chapter 58 is then narrated by the murderer. The other miniaturists attack him, and Black thrusts a needle into his eyes. He finally confesses to the murders and reveals the missing illustration. It is not a portrait of the Sultan but of the murderer himself, who feels guilty about painting a self-portrait in the Venetian style. The murderer, now revealed as Olive, attempts to flee. He attacks and injures Black and then runs out and heads for the harbor. He is intercepted by Hasan, who beheads him with his sword.

The story is completed in Shekure's voice. She nurses the wounded Black back to health. He remains melancholy but retains his interest in painting. Enishte's book remains unfinished; Stork became Head Illuminator following Master Osman's death. Butterfly devotes his life to drawing ornamental designs for carpets and tents.

Characters

Black

Black is the nephew of Enishte. In Black's youth, Enishte enrolled him at the artisans' workshop, but he preferred a bureaucratic post. When he was twenty-four, Black fell in love with Shekure, but his uncle did not consider him a suitable match, and he was asked to leave the house. He then traveled extensively. While in Tabriz, he produced books for pashas and other wealthy patrons, dealing directly with the artists. He was also in the service of various pashas as clerk or treasurer's secretary. On his travels he witnessed many battles, and he has written a history of the Persian wars that he plans to present to the Sultan. Black is a cultured man who regards himself as a connoisseur of illustrating and decoration. He returns to Istanbul at the age of thirty-six at the request of Enishte. He is still in love with Shekure and wants to marry her. Black is tall, thin, and handsome, and Enishte regards him as a determined, mature, and respectful nephew.

Butterfly

Butterfly is one of the four master miniaturists selected to work on the secret book for the Sultan. Butterfly thinks he is the best artist since he makes the most money. He enjoys his work and has recently married a woman whom he regards as the most beautiful in the neighborhood. Enishte also thinks Butterfly is the most talented artist, and says Master Osman was in awe of him for years. Master Osman confirms this in his own reminiscences, saying that Butterfly was so handsome in his youth that people could hardly believe it and took a second look. As an artist, Butterfly's strength is in applying color, and according to Master Osman, he paints from the heart. But Osman also regards Butterfly as flighty and indecisive.

Elegant

Elegant was a master miniaturist who embellished books, coloring the borders with designs of leaves, branches, roses, flowers, and birds. When he was younger, he would decorate a plate or a ceiling, but he decided to work only on manuscript pages because the Sultan paid well for them. Elegant was murdered just before the story begins. He had been afraid that the illustrated book he and the others were working on was blasphemous, and it appears that he was murdered because of fears that he would denounce the entire project to the religious fundamentalists, thus endangering everyone who has worked on it. It also appears that Elegant was greedy for money; Shekure thinks he was ugly and spiritually impoverished.

Enishte

Enishte is Black's uncle. His wife and three sons are dead, and he lives with his daughter Shekure. Enishte aspires to be a venerable elder, and he has no objection to Shekure marrying a suitable man but insists that she should remain living in his house. However, Shekure fears that Enishte would not respect a son-in-law who was willing to live in his house and would soon start to belittle him.

Enishte is a former artist who has been commissioned by the Sultan to prepare a special book of illustrations, which are to be painted in the Western style, a style Enishte admires. This brings Enishte, who does not have the standing of a master illustrator, into conflict with Master Osman, who is a traditionalist. The two men dislike each other.

After the murder of Elegant, Enishte fears that he may also be murdered because of his involvement with the controversial book. At one point he decides to discontinue his involvement with it, but quickly reverses his decision. His fear of being murdered is justified, however, since this is to be his fate, killed by the same man who murdered Elegant.

Esther

Esther is an overweight Jewish woman who roams the streets of Istanbul selling clothing. She also acts as letter courier, mediator, and matchmaker. She has few principles, and thinks nothing of reading people's letters, even though she is illiterate and has to get someone else to read them for her. She allows Hasan, for example, to read the letters Black sends to Shekure. Esther is boisterous, good-natured, and lively, with a good understanding of human nature and the ways of the world. As a Jew in an Islamic city, she is forced to wear a pink dress.

Hasan

Hasan is Shekure's brother-in-law. He is in love with Shekure and seeks to force her to marry him. For a while after Shekure's husband went missing, he and Shekure lived together. But although Shekure liked his humble demeanor, and the fact that he played well with her children, he alienated her by forcing her to do housework, and this prevented her from loving him. Hasan, although he has an aggressive, belligerent element to his personality, lacks confidence and knows that Shekure will never love him. Because of this he tries to force her to return to live with him by getting a judicial order to this effect. When Shekure marries Black, Hasan accuses her of entering into an invalid marriage, but his protests lead nowhere, although for a brief time after Enishte's murder he does persuade her to live with him. At the end of the novel, it is Hasan who kills the murderer, believing that he is one of the men who took part in a raid on Hasan's house to abduct Shekure.

Hayrire

Hayrire is a slave girl in Enishte's house. She is also his mistress. Shekure suspects that she may have had a child by Enishte and that she is maneuvering to become mistress of the house.

Nusret Hoja

Nusret Hoja of Erzurum is a fundamentalist preacher who claims that recent disasters in Istanbul, such as plagues, fires, and wars with the Persians, happened because people have strayed from the path of Islam.

Olive

Olive is one of the four master miniaturists who are working on the illustrations for the secret book. In the chapters he relates, he reveals very little about himself, although he does let slip that he is conceited about his own abilities and thinks the other artists are jealous of him. Master Osman, who has known Olive since he was an apprentice, regards him as quiet and sensitive, but also proud and wily, and the most devious of the master artists. But Osman does not believe Olive is the murderer, and he has a high opinion of his talent, commenting that Olive comes from a long line of masters. Black believes that Olive is enthusiastic about the Frankish style favored by Enishte, although nothing Olive says confirms this, until the startling revelation at the end of the novel. Olive is ultimately exposed as the murderer.

Orhan

Orhan is the six-year-old son of Shekure. He is a mischievous boy who is constantly quarreling with his older brother. Black thinks he is sensitive and astute.

Master Osman

Master Osman is the ninety-two-year-old Head Illuminator. Regarded as a great master, he is half-blind. Gaunt and bony, he admits he is short-tempered and complains about everything. His virtue is that he has devoted his entire life to art, but Enishte despises him and calls him senile because of his allegiance to the old methods and his hatred of innovation. Master Osman has similar feelings about Enishte. Master Osman loathes the idea of imitating European artists and reveres the old masters. He claims that sixty years ago he met the great master Bizhad and kissed his hand. Master Osman's knowledge is vast and he identifies strongly with the dedication and the suffering of all the artists of the past, whose lifelong labors often ended in blindness. Eventually, realizing that the world he loves is coming to an end and there is nothing he can do to stop the advance of the Venetian style, he chooses to blind himself.

Shekure

Shekure is the daughter of Enishte, with whom she lives, along with her two young sons. Shekure is twenty-four years old; she is beautiful and intelligent and knows her own worth. However, she is in a dilemma. Her husband, a military man, has gone missing in the war, and she finds herself courted by two men, Hasan, her brother-in-law, and Black. She appears to put Black off, but really she is attracted to him. Shekure is a wily woman who does not always tell the whole truth, and she is often confused about her situation, wanting the best for her children, needing to please her father, and not sure of her own affections. After her husband disappeared, she fell upon hard times and had to go to live with Hasan, who sold their slave and made her do housework that she detested. So she is unwilling to marry him, fearing that she would become his slave rather than his wife. Eventually she agrees to marry Black, although she says he must solve the mystery of the murders and finish the Sultan's book before she will sleep with him.

Shevket

Shevket is the seven-year-old son of Shekure. His grandfather, Enishte, describes him as stubborn, but Black tells Shekure he thinks Shevket is strong, honest, intelligent, and decisive as well as stubborn.

Stork

Stork is one of the four master miniaturists who is working on the secret book for the Sultan. He was the first Muslim illustrator to go on a military campaign with the army and depict the scenes of battle. Stork also acquired a reputation as one who liked to depict gory scenes. When he talks about his craft, he says he commits everything he sees to memory, and Master Osman notes how Stork observes every obscure detail. Master Osman recalls how Stork committed to paper what no one before him had been able to do, but he also regards Stork as ambitious and conceited. He is a hard worker, and if left to himself, he would make all the illustrations in the workshop himself. Although according to Master Osman, Stork's approach resembles that of the Venetians, he did not depict people's faces as individual or distinct since he did not consider faces important. Master Osman believes, incorrectly, that Stork is the murderer.

The Sultan

The Sultan appears directly only once, when Master Osman and Black are in the palace. Black is almost overwhelmed by the sight of the man and throws himself at his feet. He is struck by the Sultan's dignity and handsome appearance. The Sultan takes an active interest in the illustrations for the book, and he orders that the murderer of Elegant and Enishte be quickly found.

The Clash between East and West

At the heart of the novel is the clash between Eastern and Western methods of painting, which reflect different ways of seeing the world. The painter of Islamic miniatures followed tradition. He would imitate the work of previous masters; there was no question of cultivating originality, a personal style or an individual technique. He saw no need to sign his name somewhere in the picture. Individual creativity was frowned upon because creativity was considered the preserve not of man but of Allah.

Topics for Further Study

- Pick one of your favorite artists from

any period in history and show how his or her paintings change the way you see the world. Make a class presentation in which you present images from your selected artist. Discuss the different aspects of the artist's work that you respond to.

- Find some examples of Renaissance art, such as paintings by Giovanni Bellini or Tiziano Vecellio (better known as Titian), and compare them in detail with some examples of Turkish miniature paintings. Make a list of all the differences you see. Is it fair to say, as it says in the novel, that one style is painted from the human point of view and the other is from the point of view of God? What do those terms mean to you? Write an essay in which you explore these issues.

- Lead a class discussion about the present-day conflict between East and West. In what way is the East-West culture clash a result of different ways of seeing the world? What might those differences be? Issues you might want to cover include human rights, religion, individuality and community, democracy and theocracy, and relations between church and state.

- Write an essay in which you discuss why Pamuk uses multiple narrators to tell his story. How does this technique relate to the issue of style presented in the novel? How does it relate to the differences between East and West presented in the novel? How would the novel have been different if it had been told by an omniscient narrator? If it were to be told by one single character, which character should that be, and how would the story have been different?

The Islamic miniaturist attempted to represent the world from the point of view of Allah, from high above, so to speak, whereas the European painters of the Renaissance adopted a human point of view, developing the art of portraiture, in which every minute detail of an individual was represented. Islamic miniaturists depicted individuals in a more impersonal way. For example, Black sees an illustration at the artisans' workshop in which the Sultan's face is drawn adeptly, but "not so detailed as to permit one to distinguish Him from others by features alone." In contrast, in the Venetian style, individual portraits were clearly of one particular person and could not be mistaken for anyone else. Traditionalists such as Master Osman are appalled by this new method, which to them raises man to the center of the universe and therefore borders on the blasphemous. In the Venetian style, the painting exists for its own sake, whereas in traditional Islamic art, the miniaturists are only illustrating a story, not creating something that stands alone. The traditionalists fear that if they adopt the Venetian style, eventually the picture will become an object of worship in its own right. They are also alarmed by the use of perspective. Those who oppose the Venetian style regard it as a sin to draw a dog, a horsefly and a mosque as if they were the same size, using the excuse that the mosque is in the background. In the traditionalist view, this is an inversion of true values because it sees from the human eye rather than the eye of God. In this novel, paintings raise important religious and spiritual issues because a painting influences the way a person sees the world.

The progressives among the artists want to make use of both Western and Eastern styles. The Sultan's purpose is political (although there may be individual pride involved as well). He wants to show that the Ottomans can use the Western style as well as the Europeans, thinking that such illustrations in a book about Islamic military strength and pride will awe the Venetians and increase Ottoman power. This turns out not to be the case, since Olive admits that his attempted self-portrait in the Frankish style is crude and unsuccessful. Despite his artistic talent, he failed in his task and says it will take the Islamicists centuries to attain the same proficiency as the Venetians. What the Sultan intended as a demonstration of Ottoman power becomes instead a symbol of its impotence.

Another character who wants to make use of both styles is Enishte. He argues that the coming together of two different styles is to be welcomed and has happened before in Islamic history. He says that Persian painting was a combination of Arabic illustrating and Mongol-Chinese sensibilities. This is confirmed by Stork, who attributes the renaissance of Islamic illustration hundreds of years ago to a man named Ibn Shakir who absorbed the techniques of the Chinese masters. Stork seems to endorse the new style in his argument with Butterfly in chapter 56. Stork is determined to illustrate battles the way he has actually seen them, "a tumult of armies, horses, armor-clad warriors and bloodied bodies." When Butterfly counters that the artist must draw what Allah sees, not a confused battle scene as it appears to human eyes, but two opposing armies in orderly array, Stork replies, "exalted Allah certainly sees everything we see," which neatly justifies the presentation of a subject from the human point of view, since such a view does not of itself invalidate the divine perspective.

The futility of much of the argument on both sides is made clear by Enishte after his death, when he confesses to Allah his attraction to the Venetian art. The answer Allah gives, which Enishte recalls in his thoughts, is "East and West belong to me," an all-encompassing viewpoint that makes the disputes that drive the novel seem small and petty by comparison. In this novel of fanaticism, in which people kill over matters of art, Butterfly also reaches a sane conclusion with which the modern reader can concur: "An artist should never succumb to hubris of any kind ... he should simply paint the way he sees fit rather than troubling over East or West."

Blindness

The eventual blindness of the artist who labors all his life creating art is a recurring theme. But blindness is presented not as a tragedy but almost as a goal; instead of preventing the production of art, it actually enhances it. The idea in Islamic art is that the artist works within an established tradition, following the work of previous masters. He works not so much from direct observation of objects but from imitation of earlier works and repetition of the same methods. After many years of working in this way, the artists find that they are painting from memory, so they do not actually have to see in order to paint. Blindness also frees them from being influenced by other artistic styles and from the sensory realm and all the distractions that come with it. For example, Olive says to Black, "Blindness is a realm of bliss from which the Devil and guilt are barred." Blindness is not a disability or something to be feared; it is a reward offered by Allah after an artist has devoted his life to his work. Olive also remarks that some of the miniaturists who have become old without going blind are embarrassed by this fact and fear that it will be perceived as a lack of talent or skill. Some artists even pretend to be blind when they are not; they long to perceive the world the way a blind man does.

What an artist thinks about blindness is one of the three questions that Master Osman tells Black to put to the miniaturists. He says it will reveal how genuine a painter is. For Master Osman, blindness is "the farthest one can go in illustrating; it is seeing what appears out of Allah's own blackness." In other words, blindness helps the artist to present objects and scenes, not as they appear to men, but as they are viewed by Allah. When Master Osman spends the night poring over illustrations in the Treasury, he comes across many legends about blindness, which he refers to as "the ageless sorrow and secret desire of the genuine miniaturist." One illustration depicting a man being blinded by an arrow appears to him not as a tragedy but as a celebration. It is against this background that Master Osman's decision to blind himself must be seen. It is a mystical desire to encounter the "blessed darkness" of Allah.

Setting and Atmosphere

The novel creates a lively picture of late sixteenth-century Istanbul, a great imperial city that is going through troubled times. It has been shaken by fires and plague; military defeats against the Persians have disrupted the economy and led to runaway inflation, a situation made more unstable by the influx of counterfeit currency. The social disruption has allowed fiery conservative clerics to rise to prominence. They preach that the disasters that have afflicted Istanbul happened because people have strayed from the strict path laid out in the Koran. These preachers oppose tolerance to Christians, the sale of wine and the playing of music in the dervish houses. They also denounce the drinking of coffee as a sin that dulls the mind and causes ulcers and hernias. They want the many coffeehouses in the city, which they see as the disreputable haunts of pleasure-seekers and the wealthy, to be closed. One of the coffeehouses is frequented by the miniaturists, and they enjoy listening to the irreverent stories told there by a storyteller who mocks the conservative preachers and undermines or questions traditional attitudes towards social and religious matters. This particular coffeehouse is located in the back streets of the slave market, a reminder that slavery existed in the Ottoman Empire at this time. Enishte keeps a slave,

Hayrire, in his house.

The atmosphere of Istanbul is conveyed by characters such as Black, Enishte and the murderer as they walk through the streets of the city. Returning after a long absence, Black finds the city bigger and wealthier, but not as happy as he remembers it. It seems to be a city of extremes. He is astonished by the extravagant new houses that have been built, with expensive Venetian stained glass. But the streets seem narrow to him, and there are beggars on them, too. But despite the ominous aspects of the city, Black is entranced by its sights and sounds, which he captures in this passage as he looks down from a high vantage point:

> The cypress and the plane trees, the rooftops, the heartache of dusk, the sounds coming from the neighborhood below, the calls of hawkers and the cries of children playing in mosque courtyards mingled in my head and announced emphatically that, hereafter, I wouldn't be able to live anywhere but in their city.

Recurring Motifs

The title of the novel is a clue to the importance of the color red, a recurring motif (a motif is a recurring pattern, theme, symbol or image in a work of literature) that occurs in a number of contexts. Colors are vital to the painter and have a religious significance. Enishte speaks of "the mysteries of red ink," and the artists agree that if the Mongols had not brought "the secrets of red paint," they would not be able to produce their paintings. The Treasury itself, in which Black and Master Osman examine thousands of illustrations, is suffused with a dark red, caused by the cloth and dust in the peculiar light of the candles. Master Osman explains that the particular color red in one illustration belongs to the great master Mirza Baba Imami, who never disclosed his secret to anyone. "Allah never directly revealed this fine red except when He let the blood of his subjects flow," he says. It is only visible in the work of the greatest masters.

The connection between the painter's red pigment and human blood occurs in another context, too. When Black presents his uncle with a bronze three-hundred-year-old inkpot, he says "Purely for red." This is the same inkpot that Olive uses to kill him, which gives an ironic meaning to Black's earlier words, since the red color the inkpot produces is also the red blood of Enishte. As he dies, Enishte finds that red is the only color he sees: "What I thought was my blood was red ink; what I thought was ink on his hands was my flowing blood."

The color red also acquires a mystic significance. As Enishte's soul approaches Allah, he feels the presence of "an absolutely matchless red," and soon a beautiful red suffuses him and the whole universe:

The red approaching me—the

omnipresent red within which all the images of the universe played—was so magnificent and beautiful that it quickened my tears to think I would become part of it and be so close to Him.

The Ottoman Empire

The year 1591, in which the novel is set, was a significant date for Islam because it was the year before the thousandth anniversary of the Hegira, when the Prophet Muhammad emigrated from Mecca to Medina in 622. This date marked the beginning of the Muslim calendar. (The thousand years are lunar, not solar, years.) During this period the Ottoman Empire had just passed the zenith of its power and was beginning to face challenges from Europe (including, as the novel shows, the challenge of a new artistic style), that would eventually lead to its demise.

The Ottoman Empire had been growing in power since the Christian city of Constantinople was conquered by the Ottoman Sultan Mehmet the Conqueror in 1453. This event marked the end of the Byzantine Empire, and Constantinople, renamed Istanbul, became the capital of the Ottoman Empire. A century later, the reign of Ottoman Sultan Süleyman the Magnificent (1520-1566) ushered in what became known as the Golden Age of Ottoman Culture, in which architecture, art, and music flourished, as well as law-making and commerce. Süleyman expanded the Ottoman Empire by military conquest. He set his sights on Central Europe, even laying siege to Vienna in 1529, although the siege was not successful.

In 1571, Ottoman power was checked by a huge naval battle in the Mediterranean, at Lepanto, in which combined European forces defeated the Ottomans. However, within two years, Venice made peace with the Ottoman Sultan Selim II (1566-1574) and agreed to give up Cyprus. But this would prove to be the last great Ottoman military success, even though for the next quarter century, between 1578 and 1606, the Ottomans continued to wage war against central Europe and the Persians.

Although much of his attention was occupied by war, Sultan Murat III (1574-1595), who appears briefly in the novel, was personally interested in books and miniatures, and it was at his request that many books, including the *Book of Victories* and the *Book of Festivities* (both mentioned in the novel) were produced. The characters Master Osman and Olive in the novel are based on real historical figures living in Istanbul during this period: Osman the Miniaturist and Velijan, respectively.

Despite this flowering of artistic excellence, however, during this period the Ottoman Empire was failing to counter the emerging power of a rapidly developing Europe. According to historian Halil Inalcik, "the fundamental institutions of the classical Ottoman Empire ... disintegrated under the impact of a new Europe and the Ottomans were unable to adapt themselves to the changed conditions." The Ottomans were inward-looking and did not feel the need to learn from European ideas and technology. During the reign of Sultan

Ahmet I, for example, the large clock, a triumph of technology, which Elizabeth I of England had sent to the Sultan as a gift, was deliberately destroyed.

Istanbul

After its capture in 1453, Istanbul became the capital of the Ottoman Empire. The city grew rapidly in population as thousands of people were forcibly relocated there, and it was a cosmopolitan city, with Muslims, Greeks, and Jews comprising the three largest ethnic groups. By the late fifteenth century the population was nearly one hundred thousand people. Istanbul's buildings, including many mosques, schools and hospitals, were impressive. The Topkapi Palace, for example, built immediately after the Ottoman conquest and referred to in the novel simply as the palace, consisted of a number of buildings, gardens, courtyards and gates. The palace was the seat of government and included a throne room where the Sultan conducted official business.

The city continued to grow rapidly, reaching a population of four hundred thousand in the early part of the sixteenth century and rising possibly to around eight hundred thousand people by 1600. It was then the largest city in Europe, with excellent public services and flourishing trade. Centers of business, such as the Great Bazaar, were constructed around a bedestan, a central building with stone domes and iron doors where merchants could gather and goods could be securely stored.

Shops and places of work grew up around the bedestans. Istanbul was noted also for its coffeehouses, which, from the middle of the sixteenth century, were the centers of social life in the city. Istanbul was also noted for its public bathhouses (there were reportedly 150 of them) and its dervish monasteries or lodges, which were used for study and contemplation. (In the novel, Olive retreats to an abandoned dervish lodge where he is finally cornered by the other miniaturists.)

Compare & Contrast

- **Late 1500s:** In Ottoman society, religious fanaticism is on the rise and has been since the early part of the century. Powerful conservative clerics known as *ulema*, who interpret and execute Islamic law, denounce mysticism, poetry, music, and dancing (among other things), as being against Islam. One such *ulema* is Mehmed of Birgi (1522-1573), whose followers continue to argue his point of view in Istanbul mosques in the 1590s, causing much social upheaval.

  Today: Turkey remains populated almost entirely by Muslims, but since 1923 it has been a secular state. Religious freedoms are respected, but the government restricts any signs of religious fundamentalism, such as the wearing of headscarves by women.

- **Late 1500s:** The powerful Ottoman Empire, with its capital city of Istanbul, is often at war with the rising powers in Europe. Indeed, the Ottomans acquire the island of Cyprus in 1593, but they face increasing challenges from the rapid development in Europe.

  Today: Turkey, with its capital city of Ankara, is negotiating to join the European Union. If all obstacles are overcome, the earliest date for Turkey's membership would be 2013. One such obstacle is Cyprus, which is divided into Greek and Turkish regions. Turkey refuses to acknowledge the Republic of Cyprus, which is a member of the European Union, as the sole authority on the island.

- **Late 1500s:** Istanbul is known as a relatively tolerant city, in which Muslims and Greek Orthodox Christians live together. Immigration of Jews from Europe is encouraged.

  Today: Because of rising nationalism in Turkey, some observers raise doubts about the nation's commitment to democracy and human rights. The issues of political and religious freedoms, freedom of speech, and the guaranteed rights of minorities, such as Kurds and Christians, are factors in Turkey's negotiations to join the European Union.

Critical Overview

My Name Is Red met with unanimous praise from reviewers. A reviewer for *Publishers Weekly* admires the novel's "jeweled prose and alluring digressions, nesting stories within stories," and concludes that Pamuk will gain many new readers with this "accessible, charming and intellectually satisfying, narrative." A *Kirkus Reviews* critic describes the novel as "a whimsical but provocative exploration of the nature of art in an Islamic society. … A rich feast of ideas, images, and lore." Jonathan Levi, writing in the *Los Angeles Times Book Review*, comments that "it is Pamuk's rendering of the intense life of artists negotiating the devilishly sharp edge of Islam 1,000 years after its birth that elevates *My Name Is Red* to the rank of modern classic." Levi also notes, as other reviewers did, that the novel, although set four hundred years in the past, reflects societal tensions that can still be found in the world today. For this reason he refers to it as "a novel of our time." In the *New York Times*, Richard Eder describes Pamuk's intense interest in East-West interactions and explains some of the metaphysical ideas that permeate the novel. He also comments that the novel is not just about ideas: "Eastern or Western, good or bad, ideas precipitate once they sink to human level, unleashing passions and violence. 'Red' is chockfull of sublimity and sin." Eder also has high praise for the characterization of Shekure, which he regards as the finest in the book. She is "elusive, changeable, enigmatic and immensely beguiling." Eder concludes with this comment about how readers are likely to experience the novel: They will ... be lofted by the paradoxical lightness and gaiety of the writing, by the wonderfully winding talk perpetually about to turn a corner, and by the stubborn humanity in the characters' maneuvers to survive. It is a humanity whose lies and silences emerge as endearing and oddly bracing individual truths.

What Do I Read Next?

- Pamuk's nonfiction book, *Istanbul: Memories and the City* (2004), presents a portrait of the city in which he was raised and lived for decades. He describes the breakdown of his family and how he found his own way in the world; he captures the melancholy quality of the city and reflects on the history of the Ottoman Empire. The book contains 206 photographs.

- *The Name of the Rose*, by Italian philosopher and novelist Umberto Eco, is often mentioned as having similarities with *My Name Is Red*. The Everyman's edition (2006) contains Eco's own commentary on the novel. Like *My Name Is Red*, it is an erudite murder mystery, set in a period remote from modern times—in this case, a medieval monastery. It also includes much discussion and information about religion in the middle ages, including histories of the Catholic Church and of various sects within the Catholic Church.

- Readers intrigued by the philosophical and religious aspects of the novel might enjoy Mohammed Marmaduke Pickthall's *The Meaning of the Glorious Qur'an: Text and Explanatory Translation* (1996 edition). This is a classic, easy-to-read translation, made in the early twentieth century, of Islam's holy book, and this edition is edited in modern English by Dr. Arafat K. El-Ashi.

- Pamuk is sometimes compared to

the Italian postmodern writer, Italo Calvino. In Calvino's novel *The Baron in the Trees* (1977), Cosimo, a young eighteenth-century Italian nobleman, decides, in a protest against society, to spend his entire life living in the trees. Calvino creates a convincing world in which this extraordinary act takes place, developing historical, philosophical and political themes as Cosimo's brother narrates the story of Cosimo's life.

Sources

Eder, Richard, "Heresies of the Paintbrush," in the *New York Times*, September 2, 2001.

Inalcik, Halil, *The Ottoman Empire: The Classical Age 1300-1600*, translated by Norman Itzkowitz and Colin Imber, 1973, p. 51.

Keats, John, "Ode on a Grecian Urn," in *Keats: Poetical Works*, edited by H. W. Garrod, Oxford University Press, 1973, p. 210.

Levi, Jonathan, "The Plague," in the *Los Angeles Times Book Review*, October 7, 2001, p. 9.

Pamuk, Orhan, *My Name Is Red*, translated by Erdağ M. Göknar, Vintage International, 2002.

Review of *My Name Is Red*, in *Kirkus Reviews*, Vol. 69, No. 15, August 1, 2001, p. 1058.

Review of *My Name Is Red*, in *Publishers Weekly*, Vol. 248, No. 32, August 6, 2001 p. 58.

Further Reading

Cicekoglu, Feride, "Difference, Visual Narration, and 'Point of View' in *My Name is Red*," in the *Journal of Aesthetic Education*, Vol. 37, No. 4, Winter 2003, pp. 124-37.

> This essay focuses on the difference between Eastern and Western ways of visual narration, taking *My Name is Red* as its frame of reference.

————, "A Pedagogy of Two Ways of Seeing: A Confrontation of 'Word and Image' in *My Name is Red*," in the *Journal of Aesthetic Education*, Vol. 37, No. 3, Fall 2003, pp. 1-20.

> This essay explores the role that the confrontations between different traditions play in the resolution of the two aspects of the novel's plot, the love story and the murder mystery.

Ettinghausen, Richard, *Turkish Miniatures from the Thirteenth to the Eighteenth Century*, New American Library by arrangement with UNESCO, 1965.

> This small, inexpensive book contains twenty-eight reproductions of Turkish miniatures from books such as *Album of the Conqueror, Book of Accomplishments, Book of*

www.ingramcontent.com/pod-product-compliance
Ingram Content Group UK Ltd.
Pitfield, Milton Keynes, MK11 3LW, UK
UKHW021419090125
4034UKWH00016B/81

the King of Kings, and *Book of the Festival*.

Göknar, Erdağ, "Orhan Pamuk and the 'Ottoman' Theme," in *World Literature Today*, Vol. 80, No. 6, November-December 2006, pp. 34-38.

> Göknar discusses Pamuk's writing as a whole, including *My Name Is Red*. Because the novel focuses on the Ottoman Empire in a European context, Pamuk is able to explore his frequent practice of presenting characters who question their identities and try to establish a new way of understanding themselves through painting or writing.

Gun, Ganeli, "Heresy in Miniature—Commissioned by the Sultan to Illustrate a Book in the European Manner, a Group of Artists Treads a Dangerous Path," in *World and I*, Vol. 17, No. 1, January 2002, p. 226.

> In this review, Gun, who has translated two of Pamuk's books into English, argues that the effect of the novel is spoiled because the translation does not render the text into colloquial (everyday) English. She claims to have discovered numerous mistranslations and misreadings.